The Smokies are not the tallest mountains in North America, but they have one of the greatest varieties of plants and animals of any mountain range. The plants and animals that live in the Smokies are always interacting, or working together, with nonliving things, such as air, sun, land, and water. Therefore, the Smokies can be described as a mountain **ecosystem**, or a particular place with living and nonliving things that constantly interact. Many people visit the Smokies to experience this mountain ecosystem and to learn more about life in the mountains.

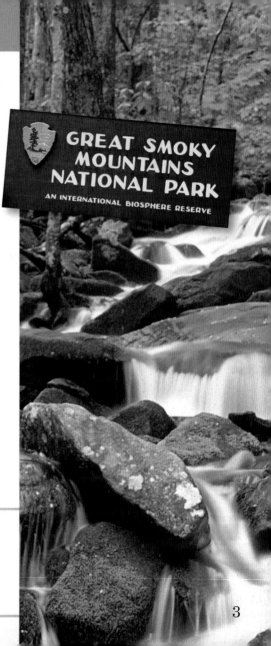

Great Smoky Mountains National Park is home to many kinds of plants and animals. People who work at the park protect the plants and the animals and help to keep them healthy.

3

Azalea

The azalea is a type of plant that grows low to the ground. The azalea's flowers bloom in the spring and are bright colors such as pink, red, yellow, and purple. The flowers usually have five petals with long, green containers around them that hold seeds. When these seeds fall to the ground, new azalea plants will grow.

Like other green plants, azaleas make their own food through photosynthesis. Azaleas use sunlight, water, and a gas called *carbon dioxide* to make food. They make sugar for energy, and they release oxygen into the air. Animals and people need oxygen in order to live.

Azelas commonly grow near the bases of large trees in Smoky Mountain forests.

Photosynthesis

Animals breathe in oxygen.

Gases combine to make sugar. Green plants turn sugar into energy, and oxygen is released into the air.

Animals breathe out carbon dioxide.

Plants use energy from sunlight to break apart other gases.

Plants absorb carbon dioxide and sunlight.

Bat

Bats are **vertebrates**, or animals that have backbones. Bats are also **warm-blooded**, which means that their bodies stay the same temperature even when the temperature of their environment changes. Bats live in caves and other dark places, and they eat mostly insects. Some people are afraid of bats, but they are very interesting animals. Bats help control the number of insects, which can sometimes be harmful to plants, other animals, and people.

Eleven types of bats can be found in the Smokies.

6

Bats' wings, like birds' wings, help them fly. Bats flap their wings and tails when they fly. However, bats are not birds—they are **mammals**. Mammal babies are born live instead of hatching from eggs, and they drink milk from their mothers.
A female bat usually has one baby each year.

The hoary bat is the largest bat. It is about 16 inches wide from wingtip to wingtip.

7

Black Bear

There are about 1,800 black bears living in Great Smoky Mountains National Park. Most black bears grow to be six feet tall and weigh between 200 and 300 pounds. Bears are furry mammals that eat mostly grasses, fruits, and nuts. However, they also eat insects, and some bears eat small animals. Black bears are called black, but they can be almost any color, including black, dark brown, light brown, gray, and very rarely, white.

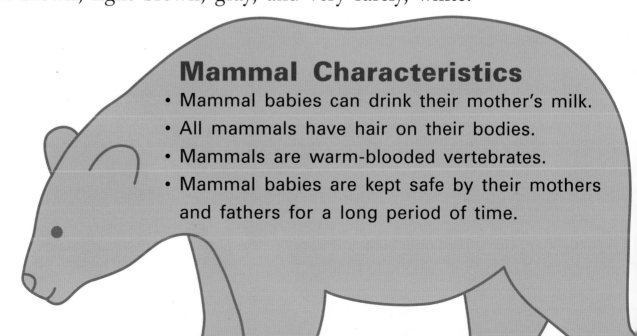

Mammal Characteristics

- Mammal babies can drink their mother's milk.
- All mammals have hair on their bodies.
- Mammals are warm-blooded vertebrates.
- Mammal babies are kept safe by their mothers and fathers for a long period of time.

8

Black bears sleep during the winter when it is cold and finding food is difficult. In the fall, black bears prepare for their winter sleep—they eat a lot of food to store fat in their bodies. They use the extra fat for energy while they are sleeping. They sleep in dens, which can be caves, hollow trees, or piles of leaves.

Female bears have one to four babies, or cubs, in the winter. The cubs leave the den with their mother in late spring.

A black bear cub learns how to do things like find food and stay safe by watching what its mother does and copying her.

9

Broadleaf Trees

There are over 200 kinds of trees in the Smokies. Trees are the largest type of plant. Like other green plants, all trees make food through photosynthesis.

Most broadleaf trees have wide, flat leaves that change colors in the fall and drop from the branches in the winter. The trees rest until spring, when new leaves grow. Some trees, called hardwood trees, have nuts that many animals eat. New trees grow from seeds made by other broadleaf trees. Broadleaf trees include maples, oaks, hickories, birches, chestnuts, ashes, and poplars.

The yellow birch has very thin bark that peels from the tree like paper.

This maple tree is a type of broadleaf tree. Its colorful leaves will fall off before winter begins.

These trees are called silverbells because they have flowers that are shaped like bells.

11

Duskytail Darter

Duskytail darters are fish that live in the waters of the Smokies. They are named for their brown tails and for their quick, darting movements. Like other fish, darters are vertebrates and use gills to breathe and fins to swim. They are also **cold-blooded**, which means that their body temperature is always the same as the temperature of their environment.

Duskytail darters live in clear streams. There are over 600 miles of streams in Great Smoky Mountain National Park.

In the late 1950s, fewer and fewer duskytails lived in the Smokies because many of the streams became filled with dirt or sand. Scientists have used the process of reintroduction to increase the population of duskytail darters in the Smokies. During reintroduction young fish are raised in a safe place. Scientists then bring the adult fish back to their natural habitat, which is the place where the duskytail darter usually lives. The adult fish have babies, and the population increases. Although the duskytail darter is beginning to make a comeback, scientists must continue the reintroduction program to make sure the fish will still be able to live in Smoky Mountain streams.

The duskytail darter appears very thin when you look at it from the front, and long and wide when you look at it from the side!

Eastern Screech Owl

Owls are birds that use long claws called *talons* to hunt prey. They also have special feathers around their eyes that help them to hunt by sending sound to their ears. As with other hunting birds, an owl's wings are shaped so that they make no sound when the owl flies. Owls are warm-blooded vertebrates, but they are not mammals because they hatch from eggs like all birds.

Owls don't build their own nests. They live in nests other birds have made, in caves, or in hollow trees.

14

The eastern screech owl lives in the Smokies. It eats small mammals, such as mice and insects. It has a large, round head, with long feathers on each side of its head that look like horns. Some birds migrate, or fly somewhere warm for the winter, but the eastern screech owl does not.

15

Elk

Elk are large mammals found in the Smokies. They are the second-largest kind of deer found on the North American continent. Male elk stand about five feet tall and can weigh up to 1,100 pounds. A male elk has antlers—a pair of bony growths on its head—that it sheds each spring, and a new pair grows during the summer. Elk usually eat grasses, twigs, and the leaves of trees.

Many elk that used to roam the Smokies died when hunters and settlers came to the area. Since 2001 elk from other parts of the country have been reintroduced in the Smokies, and as these elk have babies, the elk population will increase.

Female elk are smaller than male elk, and they don't have antlers.

Gypsy Moth

The gypsy moth is an insect that goes through a caterpillar stage as it grows. These caterpillars are very dangerous to the forests of the Smokies because they eat the leaves of trees, and many caterpillars can destroy all of a tree's leaves and kill the tree. Gypsy moth caterpillars are especially harmful to oak trees, which are a source of food and shelter for black bears. Therefore, the gypsy moth is dangerous to the animals of the Smokies as well as to the forests. Mice and other small mammals eat gypsy moth caterpillars and help keep them from doing too much damage.

Female gypsy moths are white with black markings, and males are brown.

17

Huckleberry

Huckleberry is a small plant with white, green, or red flowers. The leaves of the huckleberry plant turn red in the fall. Huckleberry plants have small, round fruit that can be red, black, or blue. Both animals and people can eat the fruit. For hundreds of years, people have made jams and jellies from huckleberries or baked the fruit into breads and pies, and huckleberries have always been a favorite food of black bears. Like other green plants, huckleberries make their food through photosynthesis.

Huckleberries are common in the forests of the Smoky Mountains.

Lichen

Lichen is a plant that grows mostly on rocks and trees. Lichen is made up of two tiny organisms, fungi and algae, that work together to make food through photosynthesis. Fungi absorb water, and algae absorb sunlight. Algae use the water and sunlight to make sugar, which fungi use for food, helping the lichen to grow. Most new lichen is formed when small cells called *spores* blow into the air and land near algae.

Lichen doesn't have roots like other plants. It holds on to rocks or trees with long threads. Lichen can be yellow, green, brown, or gray.

Needleleaf Trees

These trees have leaves that are called *needles* because they are thin and can be sharp. Because these green needles do not fall off the tree in the autumn and winter, needleleaf trees are also called *evergreens*. Some evergreens produce cones—woody objects that make seeds. These seeds fall to the ground and make new evergreen trees. Each type of evergreen has a different shaped cone and different kinds of leaves. Needleleaf trees in the Smoky Mountains include pine trees, spruce trees, firs, and hemlocks.

20

Fir trees like the
Fraser have soft
needles and cones
that stand straight up.

The red spruce has
bark that is red in
color. The cones hang
straight down from
the tree.

Carolina hemlock trees
are very hard to find.
They grow high in the
Smokies and have soft,
dark green needles.

21

Peregrine Falcon

The peregrine falcon is a blue-gray bird that can fly very quickly from high in the air to low to the ground. This is called *stooping*, and it helps peregrine falcons when they hunt for prey, which are other animals eaten by the falcon. Peregrine falcons usually eat other birds. When a falcon spots its prey, the falcon surprises it by stooping, then grabbing the other bird with its sharp talons.

Some of the animals that live in the Smokies are **endangered**. They are dying in large numbers, and there are few left.

N O P Q R S T U V W X Y Z

When settlers and hunters first arrived in the Smoky Mountains, many peregrine falcons died, and they became endangered. Many died because of pollution from chemicals used to control insects. People stopped using those chemicals. In the 1990s, peregrine falcons were successfully reintroduced. Their population has been increasing.

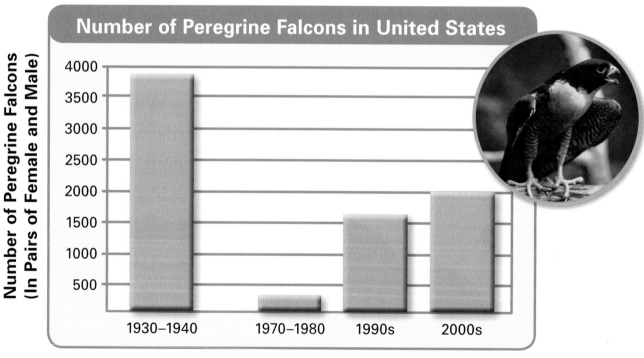

Number of Peregrine Falcons in United States

Number of Peregrine Falcons (In Pairs of Female and Male)

Time Period in Decades

Pipevine Swallowtail Butterfly

The pipevine swallowtail butterfly is an insect that goes through a caterpillar stage as it grows. Butterflies help plants when they eat. When they drink liquid called *nectar* from flowers, a dust called *pollen* sticks to their wings. Butterflies carry the pollen to the next plant and the plant uses the pollen to make seeds.

Pipevine swallowtails are named for what they eat and how they look. When they are caterpillars, they eat leaves from plants that belong to a group called the *pipevine family*. When they are adults, their back wings look like the tails of birds called *swallows*. Although pipevine swallowtail caterpillars eat plant leaves, they do not cause serious damage like gypsy moth caterpillars.

The leaves of plants in the pipevine family, such as this one, are poisonous to many animals. This protects pipevine swallowtail caterpillars from predators in the Smokies.

24

Raccoon

The raccoon is a mammal that has black rings around its tail and black fur that looks like a mask around its eyes. Raccoons have long fingers with sharp claws that help them climb trees, where they sleep during the day. Raccoons hunt at night for crabs, small animals, acorns, eggs, corn, fruit, nuts, and seeds. Most females have three to four babies each year. Mother raccoons protect their babies and don't even let the father see them until they are eight weeks old!

Raccoons are very smart and curious animals. They can use their fingers to open doors, untie knots, and take things apart. People who live in the Smoky Mountains know how clever raccoons can be.

Raccoons are intelligent animals and known to cause mischief.

25

Salamander

Salamanders are vertebrates that have tails, long bodies, and four legs. Salamanders are amphibians—cold-blooded animals that can live on land and in water. Most salamanders hatch from eggs that are laid in streams. However, adult salamanders live mostly on land. Many types of salamanders use lungs to breathe. Salamanders that belong to a group called *lungless salamanders* do not have lungs. These salamanders breathe by absorbing oxygen through their moist skin.

The Jordan's salamander can only be found in the Smokies.

26

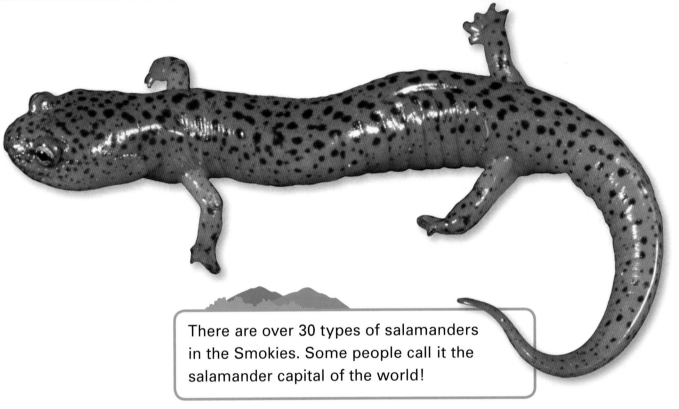

There are over 30 types of salamanders in the Smokies. Some people call it the salamander capital of the world!

Scientists pay close attention to salamander populations. Salamanders are easily affected by pollution, so if their numbers go down, scientists know that pollution may be present that can cause harm to other animals.

27

Squirrel

Squirrels are small mammals with long, furry tails. Most squirrels live in trees and use sharp claws to grab onto branches as they leap from tree to tree. They eat nuts, seeds, pine cones, and fruit. The Smokies are home to many types of squirrels, including the northern flying squirrel and the red squirrel.

To protect its nest and its food, the red squirrel gets very angry with anyone who gets too close!

28

The northern flying squirrel has a fold of skin between its wrist and ankle. This allows it to glide through the air as if it is flying. Flying squirrels can glide up to 150 feet. That's half the length of a football field!

The red squirrel will become angry if anyone gets too close to it. The red squirrel then begins to chatter loudly, jerk its tail, and dart wildly back and forth.

The northern flying squirrel isn't really flying. It is gliding like a kite by trapping air under its skin.

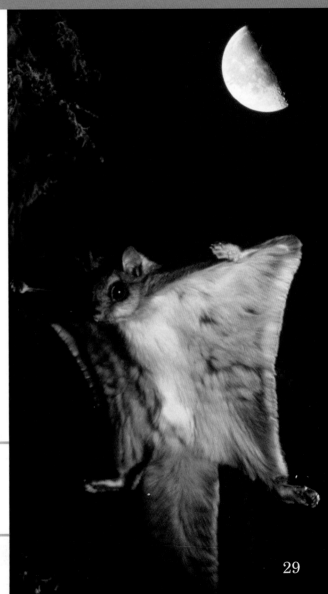

29

White-tailed deer

Deer are mammals that have antlers, like elk do. A male white-tailed deer can grow over three feet tall at the shoulders and weigh 200 pounds. This shy animal's fur is reddish-brown in the summer and turns gray in the winter. Its tail, which is brown on top and white underneath, stands straight up when the deer is frightened or in danger. Young white-tailed deer have rows of white spots on their fur. They lose the spots after a few months.

White-tailed deer eat green plants, corn, and acorns and other nuts. In June female deer have between one and three babies.

You won't have to look very far to see a deer in the Smokies. In parts of the Smokies, you can see up to 200 deer at one time!

Deer are hunted by animals such as wolves, coyotes, and bears. When a deer is in danger, it flashes its tail to warn other deer.

Yellowfin madtom

The yellowfin madtom is a type of fish that lives in warm streams in the Smokies. These fish are unusual because they are poisonous—they can sting their enemies. They also have sharp spines that extend from their fins. As their streams have become polluted, many yellowfin madtoms have not been able to survive. People who work at Great Smoky Mountain National Park are reintroducing the yellowfin madtom to the Smokies to help increase its population.

The yellowfin madtom gets its food from the beds of streams.

31

Glossary

amphibian cold-blooded animal that lives on land and in water

cold-blooded having blood that is the same temperature as the environment

ecosystem particular place where living and nonliving things interact, or work together

endangered in danger of dying off

habitat type of place in nature where a plant or animal usually lives

invertebrate animal that does not have a backbone

mammal warm-blooded, vertebrate animal that has skin, hair, and lungs; a mammal can drink milk from its mother when it is a baby

vertebrate animal that has a backbone

warm-blooded having blood that stays the same temperature in any environment

Introduction

In the southeastern part of the United States, miles of mountains covered with thick forests rise up from the ground, dividing the states of Tennessee and North Carolina. At the top of these mountains you can see a mist that looks like smoke, which is why these mountains are called the Great Smoky Mountains, or the Smokies.

The smoky mist covering the mountains is actually humid air trapped by the trees.

Great Smoky Mountains Encyclopedia

Anne Kaske, Meg Cichon García, and Heera Kang

Rigby

A Harcourt Achieve Imprint

www.Rigby.com
1-800-531-5015